AF265233

LONG STORY, SHORT.

long story, short.

LAUREN N HILL

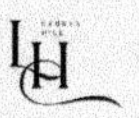

in memory of all the moments, thoughts and
promises,
good and bad,
lost and purposefully forgotten.

~ 1 ~

WHAT'S HIS NAME.

you made my mind ache
and my heart scream,
my soul burned with unfilled passion
maybe that's why it took me so long to leave;
maybe that's why i never could.

you were always the one i craved
but could never have.
i can't let go,
because my mind needs to know
and my heart needs to feel
the desires they never had.

everyone saw the fire.
it was the kind that needed put out.
i saw the ashes that were left over from
the life you had;
i would have let you burn because you kept me warm,
but your smoke was killing me.

you put your hands on me;
once i knew you it didn't scare me.
i stood there ridiculously
because i wanted to be the one person
that didn't fight you back.

why couldn't you live up to your potential?

the emotion was there, the love was there,
but the pain you caused never went away.
i waited for you, i was patient with you.
i hoped you would figure it out.
i hoped you would come home at night,
hoped you would answer my phone calls,
hoped you would tell me what was going on.
being with someone and still feeling alone is worse,

than just being alone.

have you ever tried to sleep with a broken heart?
every noise you're hoping to be a knock at the door,
a key turning in the lock.
you wake up startled but hopeful at the same time,
just to be disappointed in the morning.

the person i was scared of was the same person
i felt safe with;
i almost traded that comfort for my sanity.

i stopped liking gifts when that's what i got,
instead of your time.
lilies aren't as beautiful when they are
the most alive thing
in this one bedroom apartment.

you said you would kill me if you ever saw me out,
but for once i wasn't scared;

heaven had to be better than the hell i was living.

i hated missing phone calls because
i never knew if there
would be a next one.

no sleep was normal.
everywhere I went, I was easily startled.
always looking over my shoulder

to never feel safe.

there are only so many times you can reheat dinner
for no one to eat.
only so many times you can go to bed expecting to feel
someone beside you
to wake up to no one.
you start to question the love, the lies;

you start to question what you thought was there
and wonder
if it ever was.

it was only you.

no. it was only her and i.

[my eyes wandered around a room] *look straight.*
[that outfit complimented my body] *go change.*
[i spoke with a friendly tone] *don't flirt.*
[i left my house] *get home.*
[i answered my phone] *who's that?*

if you asked me who i was these days,
i couldn't tell you.

how could i have gotten it all wrong
when i was so sure.

i stood there looking at you, my eyes full.
i told you that my heart was breaking and i was close;
close to that door, close to walking away
and never coming back.
a tear fell down your face so for once
i thought you cared,
that you loved, that you were fighting for me.
but you left to do that same thing you did time
and time again.
the same thing that got me here.
the same thing that let me walk through that door.
alone. never to come back.

there's a beauty in walking away,
a strength in closing the door and a relief in letting go.

but i was still trying to find it.

trying to unclench your fingers from my arms,
pushing you away from me when I was
the one who fell,
waking up with bruises, struggling to find my footing
while being ripped from a bar stool,
coughing while your hands were around my neck;

sorry my bitterness isn't tasteful.

i saw you in public and my breath was taken from me.
i blinked and like a ghost you were gone.
i wish the tears left as fast as they came.
i felt the cold, it made me shiver, but this time
i couldn't
find the fire.

how can someone be out of your life for so long
and yet still hurt you so badly in your dreams?

the emotions overwhelming, the tears,
the sweat-soaked t-shirt.

i have seen your beauty and the depths of your soul:
your most gruesome scars, your most hidden tears.

i do wonder how you're doing today.

when i met you
i experienced a person
who isn't truly capable of loving another person,
and i'm not sure it's their fault.

~ 2 ~

STOP THE NOISE.

i remember a time when my thoughts were so pure.
when i thought my happiness would only be taken
if i allowed it to be.
if only i could go back to thinking like that innocent
girl
i once was.

are you ever so tired that you can't even cry?

you stop trying to care.

you feel like you're not breaking, but already broken.

being fake never seemed so hard until
i tried to smile while a war was going on inside of me.

there came a time in my life where
all i wanted
was to not feel so damn sad for no reason.

everything is so loud,
even when i don't hear anything.
i would cover my ears
but it's all coming from inside of me.

i write sometimes mad and my pencil can't keep up,
other times sad and my tears soak the page,
blurring what i have written,
as if trying to erase it off the paper,
out of my mind and my heart.
if only it all worked like that.

i just want silence.
even the whisper of music sounds like screaming.
when the sound is off, the only noise is the chaos in
my head.
i turn the music back on, because my thoughts could
kill me.

that darkness is back, my mind black as can be.
yet i see so much, too much.
i nod as if I'm paying attention to the people and
conversations around me.
i try to stay focused but that is an impossible
venture these days.
i fake a lot of what i give. i want to make it go away,
that feeling of drowning so realistic.

God, just please don't let me go. don't let the night
come.

i can't even tell those around me what's in my head.
it's too dark, too wrong,
too messed up.
what's this disease taking over my mind?
let me out.
let me breathe.
let me escape.
i reach up to pull the hands that are choking me away
from my throat
but no one is there.

i always tell people they are never too far gone.
i don't know if i'll ever believe that for myself.

i've gotten stronger, i've changed my actions,
learned to stop my mind.
but the one thing i can't fight is when i lay down at
night
and close my eyes.
the pictures so vivid, the feelings so real and
the emotions so overwhelming.
somehow it makes me weak for days.

i know there is a clear sky above me
but all i see is the fog.
if i could just get above the clouds
everything would
make sense.

do you ever feel like your emotions
create your identity?
i wake up and i'm in this glass box.
i can see everyone around me,
i can hear them talking.
i yell and no one hears me, i beat on the walls
until i'm exhausted.

there are so many emotions that i just don't feel.
i'm selfless and yet so selfish at the same time.
i've been the person that i said i would never be,
and didn't feel sorry for it.
i've apologized so many times and didn't mean it.
i've made promises i knew i couldn't keep.

i'm a mess, i'm glad no one can tell what i'm
thinking.
even though it's probably written on my face.
nevermind,
i'm too fake for that. i'm trying to get better with
that.
now i just don't talk.
i don't fake the smiles or the conversations.
i don't have the energy for that anymore.

craving vodka like i used to crave water.
just enough to get out of my head.
to let me escape for just a little while.
to feel everything and nothing at the same time.
no consequences.
passionate emotions.
real and relatable actions that only others
call mistakes.
i call them love.

i run around all day and come home out of breath.
i smile and laugh with people whose jokes aren't
funny.
i say yes when i most definitely want to say no.
i don't deal with the emotions that are overwhelming
my life.
i haven't prayed in days, like really prayed,
but yet i want saving so bad.
save me from this day to day mediocre, joyless life
i call normal.

i drive miles and miles before realizing the radio is
off, my head
has been somewhere else for quite some distance. i
don't notice
laughter or exchange smiles.

hoping that joy finds me again before i forget
what she looks like.

walking back into the shade, the warmth scares me.
when you get warm, the cold stings that much more.
i would rather stay cold.

if you painted me, i'm sure that all you would see is
black.
all the strokes that lead to nowhere. the scribbles
overlapping.
the confusion. just leave me some light so i can
eventually escape.

i try to write about other things, but i guess pain
sharpens the lead.

~ 3 ~

A COMBINATION OF TWO ELEMENTS.

we knew from the start,
we were running in opposite directions.

the passion was always there in our fighting,
just never in our love.

maybe we thought marriage was going to fix us.
we had everyone fooled except ourselves.

i was too much of one thing
and not enough of another.
i was too much myself and didn't want to be like you.
you needed me to need you and i wanted nothing
from you.
i started not to care if i was under you,
because being next to you no longer was appealing.

he asks me why i cry.
it's not from the argument we just had or the one
from last night or the week before that.
no, its from the years of telling
myself not to feel how i feel right now.
constantly letting myself down by not standing up.

i nod,
i agree.

just to lose myself a little more each time.

go ahead and tell me it's all in my head,
that i'm crazy and i make it all about me.
with all the mistakes i'm reminded of daily, trust me
i would rather nothing else be about me.

where do we go from here?
in the same spot having the same conversation
as last week and the week before.
i whisper i'll do better,
that i'm trying.
words that aren't foreign.

tears that are as common as a smile.

how can i get anywhere with you when
all you remember
is the subpar version of me? i guess i can't blame you.
i know how hurt feels.

when did i lose myself? was it when i was
at fault for feeling, or when "i understand" and
"yes i agree" became part of my daily responses?

was i a pushover?

no, i was just a girl who was sick of fighting
every damn day.

suffocating again from
all the things

i can't feel

and

all the words

i can't say.

yell at me,
scream at me
until i feel nothing but your hot breath on my face.
grab me and shake me until i get out of my own head.
at the end of it all,

i'll still say i'm sorry.

i spent so much time trying to say everything
the right way, i don't know if i ever actually said
anything.
i guess not much has changed.

people asked me when things changed between us.
the thing is,
nothing changed.
this was always us. that was the problem.

~ 4 ~

YOU.

i've drunk too much.
i've said things i shouldn't have.
i've loved.
i've lost.
i've lied.
i hide.
i don't want attention, but i want yours.

i hope you,
are the last you i write about.

your voice was like music; soft and sweet,
pleasing to me.
i always pictured your eyes and could
feel the warmth
of your body.
you calmed my madness, the voices in my head
no longer so loud.
i hadn't heard silence in a long time.

i look into your eyes and i feel like i know every
part of you,
like an ocean i'm sucked deep into your soul,
feelings i can't explain nor do i want to try.

you do things to me that no one else can do.
how badly i just want to sit across the table from you
and know what you're thinking.
just to be in your presence
and know that your touch is an option.
that's where i want to live.

how can you be so far away and yet
still feel my sadness?
it's like i've known you my whole life
and yet i've just met you.

you, you were different.
a connection so real and so deep from a dream.
i could have sworn i would wake up to you in the flesh.
able to roll over and feel you.
to run my hands over you while you slept.
i go to bed hoping i'll find you there again.
disappointed every morning
when i only feel cool sheets under my hand.

we could talk but we didn't have to.

you and i love so well but we stay
so close to the top of the water.
too scared to swim away from the shore
or under the ropes.
not risking anything to feel it all.

you got a way with body language.

i can't help but watch you from across the room,
standing so confidently.
your gaze meets mine.
you smirk when you notice...

i've been watching you this whole time.

i want you in all capacities, to consume every sense.
let me feel, smell and taste you.

i watch your eyes and where they go,
what they look at.
how your face changes, when your expression
tells a story.
i read your body just to know more of you.
what excites you, what makes you nervous?
   i don't want you to tell me.
   i want to solve you like my finest mystery.

i love waking up and seeing remnants of last night
with tired eyes,
a reminder of how sweet the time was
and no longer worried about the late night.

just a pure love.

with sunrises and sunsets i don't feel
as far away from you.

~ 5 ~

HER.

in the chaos i am focused, in the silence i am broken.

i knew before it happened i didn't want it to,
that it was wrong.
i was lonely in a world where i should have had it all.
i traded my self worth for a night of feeling
anything but alone.

the lust, the craving was always there.
that's why i went back to it.
i didn't know you and you didn't know me.
you can't see the hurt if you don't stick around.
maybe that's what i liked; someone who saw
all my sunshine and none of my storms.

not being able to commit to one person didn't seem
like a bad thing,
i just wanted them to feel what i could give
and hoped that i would feel that same gift from them,
but i never did.
i just didn't know i was looking in all the wrong
places.

sharing a dirty martini with my mind and a glass of
whiskey
with my heart.

oh, how they are always different.

i miss the times when what i hid was under my
clothes,
not in my head and heart.

on the outside she's strong, fierce and to some, sexy.
on the inside she's broken, living in darkness.
remembering how she got here is something she
wishes she could forget.

i saw the blue sky through the fog and its warmth hit
me,
i had the slightest bit of hope and started to feel.
i was thawing, no longer so numb.

i wasn't lonely anymore.
no longer needy, i didn't want you to want me.
i was comfortable, content.
the old me was fading.
it was easier to fly alone.

~ 6 ~

HORIZON.

feeling alive and free at the same time is like
nothing i can explain.
the joy that comes from feeling the sun on your skin
and the cool breeze across your face:
that's heaven on earth.

tears start to fill my eyes, that feeling is back again.
i'm frustrated to feel the heaviness in my chest,
the lump in my throat.
i felt God cover me with his warmth
as i sit on the porch rocking chair.
usually when i get to this place i cry
because that is what makes me feel normal again.
today it was the sunshine.

i thank God. is this what true joy feels like?
to be able to lie down and take a deep breath.
to feel my heart beating and know that
it's not because of panic,
but because i'm alive.

how did i get here?
i need to know so i can always find my way back.
back to this peace, back to this comfort.
back to this joy and back to this love.
this place that i felt wasn't a part of me.
but you always were.

i stand there, in a new place.
a place that is now my home.
the sun shines through the stained glass window
and i know that this is where i'm supposed to be.
in this warmth is where i feel close to you.

i want to sit in the dark a little bit longer.
holding my warm coffee between my hands
on a bar stool.
i hear nothing, not even the thoughts in my head,
a rarity.
while the world around me sleeps i can believe
that this peace,
this calmness is a way of life.
if only before the sun rises.

sometimes i just want to run away,
not from something but to something.
to new experiences,
new love and a
new peace.

sometimes we think all the chapters in our life
are going to come together to make one
happy ending,
but then we live each chapter
and start to wish some of them didn't exist.

there are no restarts.

where we are and how we got here
comes from all the pieces,
not just some of them.

all the mess and brokenness make us that
much more beautiful.

while i was searching for home,
I had gone to a place far away
that couldn't be seen in any distance.
a place where worldly influence takes over,
where my mind couldn't rest and my soul
wasn't at peace.
i had to come back home to be back in your arms,
where i could breathe again,
where the sun takes away my numb body
and light lets me see clearly.
a place where only you know me.

i'm painting wildflowers
knowing how thick the weeds are.

JUST THE BEGINNING.

98

He kept me from drowning and he taught me how to
swim | thank you to the one that saved my life.
To my biggest fan | I love you and thank you for
always supporting me.

Throughout all this I found myself.
Saved by grace.

i love roses best when they start to die.
how much more beautiful is something
with depth and dimension?
like a piece of artwork in a gallery, i sit and wonder at the
elegance,
at the journey.